Narrative and Confessions of

Lucretia P. Cannon

". . .the child continuing its cries, she caught it up and held its face to a hot fire, and thus scorched the child to death in her own hands, burning its face to a cinder. . ."

Page 14.

Narrative and Confessions of

Lucretia P. Cannon

WHO WAS TRIED, CONVICTED, AND SENTENCED TO BE HUNG AT GEORGETOWN, DELAWARE, WITH TWO OF HER ACCOMPLICES.

An account of some of the most horrible and shocking murders and daring robberies ever committed by one of the female sex.

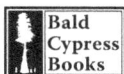

Bald
Cypress
Books

Published by
Bald Cypress Books
Laurel, Delaware

baldcypressbooks.com

Cover design and layout by Christopher Slavens.

ISBN: 978-1-7361370-4-8

Publisher's Cataloging-in-Publication Data

Names:
Title: Narrative and confessions of Lucretia P. Cannon.
Description: Reprint edition. | Laurel, DE: Bald Cypress Books,
2021.
Identifiers: ISBN: 978-1-7361370-4-8
Subjects: LCSH: Cannon, Lucretia P.,   - 1829. | Cannon, Patty,
-1829. | Criminals—Delaware—Sussex County—Biography. |
Slave trade—Delaware —Sussex County. | Kidnapping —
Delaware—Sussex County.

Front cover image: Illustration published in the first edition in
1841; public domain.

*Note: Although the first edition was registered by Clinton Jackson and
Erastus E. Barclay, it is not known whether they wrote the text.*

Narrative of
Lucretia P. Cannon

It has probably never fallen to the lot of man to record a list of more cruel, heart-rending, atrocious, cold-blooded, and horrible crimes and murders, than have been perpetrated by the subjects of this narrative, and that too in the midst of a highly civilized and Christian community; and deeds too, which for the depravity of every human feeling, seem scarcely to have found a parallel in the annals of crime.

And it seems doubly shocking, and atrocious, when we find them committed by one of the female sex, which sex, have always been esteemed, as having a higher regard for virtue and a far greater aversion to acts of barbarity, even in the most abandoned of the sex, than is generally found in men of the same class. And we can truly say, that we have never seen recorded, a greater instance of moral depravity, so perfectly regardless of every virtuous feeling, which should inhabit the human breast, as the one it becomes our painful lot to lay before our readers, in the accounts and confessions of Lucretia Cannon, the subject of this thrilling and interesting narrative. And we will now proceed to state the facts as they have actually transpired, and our readers may rely upon the accounts as being correct, as they have been gathered from the most authentic sources.

L. P. Hanly, the father of the subject of this narrative, was the son of a wealthy nobleman—residing in Yorkshire County, in the northern part of England, although he had in the early part of his life received a very liberal education, yet in consequence of being disappointed (by his father's refusing to comply with his request) in marrying the object of his first love, he fell a prey to that soul destroying monster Intemperance, and in a fit of partial derangement brought on by grief and intemperance, he married secretly, a woman who by her intrigue and artfulness, had succeeded in drawing his affections towards her, and who was also very remarkable for the influence which she exercised over the minds of men, as will be seen by referring to circumstances which occurred subsequently, for by her great tact and artfulness she succeeded in marrying her daughters (four in number) to persons of respectability, although they were every one of them prostitutes of the most common character, on this and many other similar accounts she was considered by weak and superstitious persons a witch.

Soon after this, his marriage becoming known to his father, whose indignation and anger became so great that he had determined to cut him off without a shilling, and forbade his ever after entering beneath his roof.

Matters had now come to such a pass that he determined to leave his native country, and his wife concurring in the plan, soon scraped up her effects (for she was possessed of a small estate of her own) and turned them into money, they then embarked on board one of his majesty's ships bound for Montreal, where he settled down, and for several years gained a comfortable livelihood by his industry, but as his family increased and their means of living began to grow rather scanty, his evil of intemperance also daily gaining upon him, he forsook all honest courses of getting a living, and joined a gang of smugglers, removing from Montreal to the village of St. John's situated on the St. John's River, about thirty miles from Montreal, and here carried on a regular course of smuggling between Montreal and Plattsburg, New York, and Burlington, Vermont, sometimes going as far as Quebec to obtain articles which they could not readily obtain in Montreal, and as his house was situated at a convenient distance from these places, they made it a receptacle for their goods until such time as they should find a convenient opportunity to run them in and dispose of them.

While things were going on in this style, it so happened that an old acquaintance, whose name was Alexander Payne, moved from Montreal and settled in the same neighbourhood in which Hanly resided, and as they had formerly been on intimate terms the acquaintance was soon renewed, though not with much satisfaction—on the part of Hanly, as he knew Payne to be a man of very sober and honest habits, and not likely to be easily persuaded to forsake the path of virtue; and it was on this ground and the fear of detection and exposure that Hanly dreaded again becoming on any intimate terms with his old acquaintance, for Payne was as yet entirely ignorant of the business Hanly was following, for he (Hanly) had always managed (through the influence of his wife) to keep up the appearance of honesty and respectability during his stay at Montreal.

As Payne happened frequently at the house of Hanly, he soon began to suspect that all was not right. However, he said nothing on the subject, until one evening he happened to be passing by Hanly's house rather late, and seeing, as he thought, an uncommon stir going on at that late hour he determined on going in, in order to satisfy his doubts as to what he had before suspected, and there he found Hanly and two or more of his gang secreting goods which he knew had been either smuggled or stolen. He therefore at once threatened to expose them immediately. Hanly then tried every means of persuasion in his power to induce Payne to join him in his unlawful pursuits. But all in vain, as Payne said that his duty to his God and his country, would be the instant exposure of their mis-doings. Hanly finding that he could not induce Payne to join him at any rate, he then had recourse to stratagem.

He begged of Payne to allow him but three days to settle up his affairs, and leave the country, swearing in the most solemn manner and calling upon his God to witness, that if he would grant him this request, that he would immediately leave off his dishonest course of living and forever after become an honest man. All this he said in such an earnest manner, and Payne seeing that it would also be the utter ruin of his (Hanly's) whole family, as well as himself, at length yielded to his request, after the most solemn assurances that Hanly would do as he had sworn.

But we shall now see how well he regarded his oaths and promises, for no sooner than Payne had left the house, he called in his companions and held a consultation as to what should be done, meanwhile the bottle was circulated freely, so as to steel their hearts and fit them for any fiendish purpose that should suggest itself to their maddened brains, and before they separated they determined (as their only chance of escape and evading the law) to murder Payne; they then separated for the night, resolving to meet early the next day, and lay the plan for their diabolical and fiendish purpose which was as follows.

It was agreed that they should meet near Payne's house about dark or soon after, and endeavour by some means to entice him away from his house, towards the river, when they were to fall upon him and kill him with weapons they should provide for the purpose, then they were to tie a large weight around his neck and throw his body into the river. Accordingly they repaired to their place of rendezvous at the appointed time, each one armed for the diabolical purpose with some deadly weapon, after waiting for some time without being able to see or hear any thing of Payne, (for he happened to be away from home and did not return until late) they repaired to a low public house near by, to consider what should now be done, as they were frustrated in their previous design, they here drank deeply and urged on to desperation by the maddening and intoxicating draughts they had taken, resolved upon the death of their victim at all hazards.

After disguising themselves as much as possible, they went back again to Payne's house, and finding they had returned, stationed themselves one on each side of the house, to give the alarm if they were likely to be discovered. Hanly then entered the house and groping his way through the dark until he came to the room where Payne and his wife slept, Payne hearing the door of the room open, raised himself a little in the bed, and inquired who was there, when Hanly raised an axe he had picked up outside the door and struck Payne upon the head, nearly burying it to the socket, splitting his head in a most shocking manner. He then threw down the axe and drew a large butcher's knife and rushed upon him stabbing him to the heart, and cutting his throat from ear to ear, and otherwise mangling the body in a most horrible manner, during this time Payne's wife was screaming as loud as possible for help, but Hanly paid no attention to her cries, intent only upon the death of his victim. His companions outside fled upon first hearing her cries, but persons immediately gathering around, Hanly was taken just as he was coming out of the house, he was carried directly before a magistrate, tried, convicted, and sentenced to be hung. Had he himself fled after striking the first blow with the axe, he too might possibly have escaped, but he was probably too much intoxicated. Thus some means is always left whereby the guilty are sooner or later brought to punishment. It was while on the gallows just before he was swung off, that he made his confession in very near the words above stated. His companions were afterwards taken and sentenced to prison for life for being accessory to the murder.

After the execution of Hanly his family as may be supposed, was thrown into the utmost confusion; and it was at this time that Mrs. Hanly saw the necessity of bringing all her artfulness into action, as she had now a large family dependent upon her for support, and her means of living had now become very limited, however, she managed so as to make her house a house of entertainment for persons travelling for pleasure, or those who were spending the summer months in that cool and delightful region, away from the more unwholesome air of a crowded and pent up city. And in this manner, as may be supposed, she formed many new acquaintances, and by keeping up appearances pretty high, and teaching her daughters well the arts of deception she soon succeeded in marrying them all to persons of considerable respectability. She had also an only son who was now nearing the age of manhood, and who by his long associating himself with a set of low, drinking, gambling, and licentious persons, was little better even at this age than a perfect sot, but of him we shall speak in another page.

The youngest daughter whose name was Lucretia, and which is the subject of this narrative, was, at the age of sixteen, married to a man whose name was Alonzo Cannon, a respectable wheelwright from the lower part of Delaware, who happened to be travelling through that section of country, stopped for a day or two at St. John's, where he was taken sick, and as he had put up at the house of Mrs. Hanly, and she finding her guest to be a man of very good personal attractions and possessed also of considerable money, determined at once, if possible to bring about a marriage between him and her daughter, consequently he was treated with the utmost care and attention during his illness, and Lucretia being his constant and daily attendant, also being an uncommonly agreeable person and by no means bad looking, although rather large. She was extravagantly fond of music, and dancing, a great talker, very witty and fascinating in her conversation, and concealing her real character so well that he soon fell in love with her, and her mother also exerting her influence over him he was induced to marry her immediately on his recovery.

He then returned to Delaware taking his wife with him and settled down on the Nanticoke River near the Maryland line about ten or twelve miles from Lawrel, where he established a ferry now known by the name of Cannon's Ferry, also working occasionally at his trade whenever opportunity presented.

He had not been married long as may be supposed before he found out the real character of his wife, which so preyed upon his constitution, that his health soon began a rapid decay, and at the end of three years he died, as many supposed from grief, but it has since been ascertained by her own confession that he died from the effects of a slow poison, which she had administered to him, thinking no doubt that if she was rid of him, she would then be able to carry out any plan she might devise, for the gratification of her selfish propensities—for she was very sensual in her pleasures, and totally incapable of appreciating that high toned moral feeling, and the true dignity, self respect, and refinement which should govern the female sex. She was almost indifferent to any principle of justice, as well as to human suffering; she was bold, revengeful, courageous, cunning, and determined in the objects of her pursuits, she was also very deceitful, shrewd and artful in laying her plans, which enabled her to exercise an extensive influence over the lower order of minds.

After the death of her husband she became one of the most abandoned and notorious of women, giving loose to every species of licentiousness and extravagance, and there was no crime too great, no deed too cruel, for her to engage in to accomplish any object of her design, often engaging personally in acts of the most outrageous butchery and robbery.

After living in this manner for some time she moved from

her place of habitation down near Johnson's cross roads, on the line between Maryland and Delaware, five miles from her old place of habitation, and here set up a low tavern as she knew she would there have a much greater chance of carrying on her unlawful and wicked practices. Here she made use of a great variety of artifices, to induce slave dealers and others, whom she thought likely to have any quantity of money with them, to put up with her, and she was considered by some, a very hospitable woman seldom charging her visitors anything. She so managed matters as to make her house a kind of head quarters for slave dealers, who generally had plenty of money, and soon got around her a gang of ruffians who were perfectly obedient to her will and ready to do the most bloody act when she commanded and planned it. Of this gang she was always the master spirit and the deviser of ways and means—whenever travellers, slave dealers, or others called upon her, she marked her man and at once laid her plans and train of means then gave the watchword, and often becoming the leader herself in some of the most horrible murders.

On one occasion a gentleman from Richmond (Virginia) was going to New York, and passing by her house stopped to feed his horse, and called for dinner, she finding he had a large quantity of money by him placed her unsuspecting guest at table so that his back was near an open window through which he was shot, by one of her accomplices, they then robbed him of every thing of value that he had about him, and then secreted the body in the cellar until night when they dug a hole in a side hill near the house and buried him.

At another time two slave dealers called for their dinners, she finding they also had money with them, engaged them in conversation and whiled away the afternoon by exciting and gratifying their feelings by her wit and fascinating conversation. Three several times they called for their horses and carriage which were at length tardily brought, but another glass of wine was passed around and they enticed to stay a little longer. Thus she kept them till dark, when they started for Lawrel, which was fifteen miles distant (via.) Cannon's Ferry, no sooner had they departed than she dressing herself in men's attire with three of her gang mounted on some of their fleetest horses, started in pursuit, determined on killing and robbing them. And by taking another route crossed the river above Cannon's Ferry, laying obstructions in their road as it passed up a sandy hill, and here they laid in wait for them. Stationing themselves in a convenient place to fire upon them as they came up the hill, accordingly as soon as they approached near the top of the hill, she and her gang rushed out and fired upon them, mortally wounding one so that he died in a few hours, and so frightening the travellers' horses that they ran away from both robbers and driver. But the other one though wounded managed to drive safely through to Lawrel that night, his companion died almost immediately on arriving at the inn.

One of the names of this gang was Griffin, who was afterwards executed for murder, at Cambridge, (Maryland,) and when brought upon the scaffold declared that although positively not guilty of the murder for which he was about to be executed, still acknowledged that he deserved to die because he had committed many murders, and before he was swung off he begged for a little time, as he said he wished to make a full confession of the murders he had committed and pray to God to have mercy on his soul, as he said he could not bear the thoughts of appearing before his eternal judge without confessing to the world the awful crimes of which he was guilty; he then proceeded as follows:

I was born, said he, in Cumberland County, Maine, where I lived with my father until I became seventeen years of age, when an uncontrollable desire for travel seized me. I then left my father's house and strolled about from place to place, associating myself with idle and dissipated company and by this means soon became one of the most idle and dissolute wretches in existence, in this manner I roved about and finally went to Philadelphia, here I fell in with a young man whose name was Hunt, a low gambling thieving sort of a fellow. We agreed to join companionship and share equally in whatever we should make, we then commenced by keeping a sharp look out, and whenever we discovered a man intoxicated after night, or one we thought possible to make so, we enticed them into some dark alley or other secret place and robbed them of whatever money, watches, and sometimes clothing, they happened to have with them. At length we began to grow bolder and frequently waylaid persons whom we thought had money, knocking them down, robbing them, and leaving them insensible; at one of these times we waylaid a traveller, rushed upon him endeavoring to knock him down, but the blow missing its aim, he made a desperate resistance nearly overpowering us, when drawing a large knife which I always carried about me, I stabbed him in the back; when he fell exclaiming I am murdered, we then robbed him and took to our heels. I seeing the murder advertised publicly the following morning, thought best to leave the city for fear of detection, I then went to Balti-more, dressing myself in good style endeavouring to play the gentleman. I here became enamoured of a very pretty young lady whose name was Elizabeth Morton, whose father was a respectable merchant of that city. She received my addresses very cordially for some time but at length began to suspect I was not exactly what I pretended to be, and began to grow daily more cold and reserved in my presence. I then tried to persuade her to elope with me, but this she at once refused, declaring that she would never marry against the will of her parents. Finding that I could not induce her to accede to any of my plans, I then determined on her ruin. I persuaded her to accompany me in a short ride for pleasure and conducted her to a house of ill repute, called for a room desiring that we might not be disturbed. I then locked and bolted the door, while she perceiving inquired why I did this, I then told her what my intentions were, promising her at the same time that if she would consent to marry me before returning to her father's house that I would desist, this she flatly refused, saying at the same time that she would sooner die than ever permit herself to be led to the altar by me after taking such a dishonourable course with her; she then attempted to escape but finding I prevented her, she began to cry out for help, which so enraged me that I caught up a towel hanging in the room and tried to force into her mouth; she resisting with all her might, I then twisted it around her neck, choking her until she was insensible. I then accomplished my hellish purpose, and knowing that if she should recover she would immediately expose me, I therefore resolved on her death which I consummated by tying a pockethandkerchief around her throat so tight as to prevent the possibility of her breathing. I then left her and made my escape from the house unperceived, and fled from the city intending to go to New

Orleans or some other southern city, but happening to fall in with one of Lucretia Cannon's gang, I was induced to join them which I did, and was one of the four that committed the murder (before mentioned) of the slave dealer, and that he had been accessory to several other murders, and that Lucretia Cannon was dressed in men's clothes and was their leader and most active operator.

She now moved from her old stand and enlarged her business by adding to it that of negro buying, carrying on a regular business in slave dealing, about this time two more joined the gang whose names were Johnson and Bowen, they now fitted out a slaver which used to go to Philadelphia and decoy blacks on board and when full to sail to a convenient point and send them to Lucretia Cannon's head quarters there to be shipped on board another slaver which plied up and down the Chesapeake, to be transported south. Their plan of operation was this:

They employed a very intelligent negro whose name was Ransom to prowl about the city, giving him plenty of money, mingling with the blacks, treating them freely, and by various pretences entice the unsuspecting blacks on board their ship when the hatches were closed upon them and they chained, thus half a dozen negroes would sometimes be secured in the course of a single night. They had also an old wench in their employ who kept an infamous house in a low street down near the navy yard, who also used to prowl about the city and use all the inducements in her power to entice young negroes of both sexes to come to her house, harbouring them free of charge, thus her house was always thronged with a set of lewd and dissolute negroes. It was here that Ransom always went and as he always treated them freely, he soon became a great favourite there, and as he had always some pretence on hand he seldom ever went on board without one or more of these unfortunate wretches. Towards morning the slaver would move down the bay and return the next night to go through the same process until she was loaded.

If they discovered during the day any one among their unfortunate captives, that was too old, decrepit, or infirm, which would not be worth transporting, they would throw them overboard and drown them, the rest were taken to Lucretia Cannon's as before mentioned, if any of these female negroes had children that were troublesome or likely to expose her by crying, she had a rattan with a large bullet fastened at the end of it which she would strike into their heads and thus dispatch them. She had a secret cave or dungeon dug in her cellar where she always buried these innocent victims to her savage barbarity.

On one occasion one of the negro women had a little child about five years old sometimes subject to fits, and in these fits the child used to scream in a terrible manner. It happening to have one of these fits while in Lucretia Cannon's house, she became so enraged upon hearing its cries, that she flew at the child, tearing the clothes from off the poor victim of her wrath, beating it at the same time in a dreadful manner; and, as if this was not enough to satisfy her more than brutal disposition, the child continuing its cries, she caught it up and held its face to a hot fire, and thus scorched the child to death in her own hands, burning its face to a cinder, she then threw it in the cave in the cellar.

At one time, a traveller put up for the night, intending to start early on the following morning, as he had a long days' drive to reach home before dark, which he wished to do, if possible, as he had been absent from his family for some time, but she determined this should never happen; and while he was at supper, she came behind him, and plunged a large dagger to his heart, killing him instantly. At this time, she had liked to have been discovered by some travellers entering the house at the time, but she nothing daunted, caught him up, (being a man of small stature,) and threw him on the table among the dishes, covering him up with a table cloth, and catching the whole together, thrust them into a large chest standing in the room, where she left him until they had departed, then calling in a couple of her accomplices, they then robbed him and took his body in a small boat out into the middle of the river and threw it overboard with a large stone attached to it, to prevent it from rising.

At another time, a slave dealer called at her house with two valuable slaves, intending to take them to Norfolk, (Virginia,) but a heavy shower of rain coming on, he was induced to stay all night. She put him in a room separate from the main part of the house to sleep, and during the night, she entered the room by a secret way with one of her gang, armed with a large knotty club, prepared for the purpose, without being discovered by him, and fell upon the unsuspecting sleeper, beating his head until his brains strewed the floor; they then robbed him of what money he had with him, as well as a fine valuable gold watch. They then concealed the slaves in the cellar for upwards of a week, barely giving them food enough to sustain life, she then sent them on board a slaver which happened to be on the coast bound for the south, and sold them. The body of the murdered man they buried in the garden back of the house in a secret place beneath some old rubbish.

At another time, she murdered a negro boy fifteen years of age, whom she feared would expose her. The boy had been in the house for nearly a year, in the capacity of waiter or servant, and her misdoings had always been kept a secret from him, as they were always performed while he was either absent or asleep, until the savage and brutal act of her burning the child; this he heard immediately after it was committed, from one of the negroes that witnessed the horrid deed; he then declared if this was true he would immediately run and give information to some people living near by, he then started off with this intention, but she discovering him running at some distance from the house suspected something wrong, and immediately sent a man to fetch him back, which he succeeded in doing before the boy had time to give any information, although he ran as if for his life, and declared when taken, that if ever he should get an opportunity he would inform against them. As soon as he was brought into the house, she asked him why he was running away, and upon his answering her the same as he had answered the man, she flew at him catching up a large fire shovel beating him within an inch of his life; she then took him down into the cave in the cellar, and locked him up among the dead bodies and skeletons of the children she had before murdered, leaving him in that loathsome place for upwards of two whole days and nights without a single drop of water to cool his thirst, and nothing but the cold damp earth to lie upon, during this time he had nearly perished. She then came down to see if he was still alive and finding him to be so, brought him down some cold victuals and a little water, which he devoured instantly. She then asked him if he would now inform against her if she would take him away from the dungeon. The boy declared that he would; she then caught up a stone lying on the ground, beat him to death, and left him lying in the cave.

It was about this time that she received the news of the death of her mother, and also the death of her only brother, whose name was James, who was hung but a short time before at Kingston, (Upper Canada,) for horse stealing. He had continued his riotous and dissipated course of living for some time after the marriage of Lucretia, and finally joined a gang of horse thieves and counterfeiters which infested the country round about the lakes. This gang had a regular line of communication established from Detroit through to Toronto and Kingston and across to the states, clear through to New York and Philadelphia. It is supposed that at one time before the gang was broken up there was upwards of a hundred men engaged in it, although the exact number has never been ascertained—the way they managed was this—a horse was stolen by one of the gang, and run by night to the next station and exchanged or left, and the next night run to another station, the men always returning immediately to prevent suspicion. In this way they managed until they got out of the way of pursuit. They had regular stations where they kept the horses thus stolen until they had collected a sufficient number, when they were taken in small droves to New York, Philadelphia, or otherwise disposed of. The route which James was stationed on was between Kingston and Toronto near Coburg, where he had been engaged in this manner for some time. One time he had been to Kingston with a horse thus stolen and here received a considerable sum of money for his services to the company and on his way home he broke into the stable of a British officer, and stole a very valuable horse, but the noise he made awakened an old domestic who got up and perceiving the door of the stable open went and found the horse missing and giving the alarm to the officer, several men were sent out in pursuit. He was overtaken before he had got ten miles from the place where the horse was stolen, they brought him back to Kingston where he was tried before a magistrate and thrown into prison, until the sitting of the King's Court where he was condemned and sentenced to be hung. He was executed at Kingston sometime late in the year eighteen hundred and twenty-eight.

After hearing this news she became, if possible, still more cruel and barbarous than before; she now seemed to take no delight whatever in anything but acts of the most blood thirsty and inhuman nature; nothing now satisfied her murderous disposition but the death of some innocent, and to her, unoffending victim, but her career of guilt was nearly run. She had carried it in such a high-handed and impious manner that it was impossible to continue in this way much longer without being overtaken by justice, and it was not long after this that she was by the following circumstances exposed, and her gang broken up, and nearly all of them brought to justice, for the high-handed and outrageous crimes they had long been committing and had thus far escaped detection.

She had but a few days before she was taken, murdered a traveler who was known to have put up at her house, and had never been seen or heard of after the time he entered her door, and as he was known to have had a large quantity of money in his possession at the time, suspicion therefore was strong in the neighbourhood that he had been robbed and murdered by her and her gang, as they had now become very notorious in the neighbourhood for their wickedness. However, nothing certain was ascertained about the matter for upwards of a week, when suspicion became so strong that some neighbours determined on searching the premises secretly, in order, if possible, to find out something more satisfactory concerning the matter, as well as to satisfy themselves as to what was going on about the house, for they had suspected for some time previous, as there was almost constantly some of her gang there, and they never appeared to have any other business on hand, but loitered about exciting the suspicions of the neighbourhood.

So, accordingly, they went one afternoon and visited the house, making some pretence for the visit, one of them saying that he was about to build himself a new house and begged of her permission to examine her house and take a drawing of the plan on which it was built, saying that he wished to build after the same manner, she not suspecting anything allowed them the privilege, though not permitting them to enter the cellar, they then made such examinations as they were able, discovering however nothing above, to confirm them in their suspicions which were now directed entirely to the cellar and in her absence from the room for a moment, they questioned an old wench as to what was kept in the cellar. She replied that she dare not tell for fear she would be killed; they promised to liberate and protect her if she would disclose to them what she knew about the matter, and she replied that there was something awful in the cellar, but for the life of her she dare not tell what it was. Her mistress coming in again at that instant, prevented any further discourse with her. They then left the house concluding that they had now gathered information enough to convince them that it would now be their duty to inform the proper authorities and have the house searched. Accordingly early the next morning a warrant was placed in the hands of the sheriff, who started with a party of about a dozen men armed for any emergency that might happen. Upon arriving at the house and arresting her, she resisted desperately; but seeing the party that surrounded the house was strong and well armed, and that resistance would have been instantly fatal, she and her gang surrendered. They were taken to Georgetown to be tried where one of the company, a young man who had been enticed into the service, turned states evidence and disclosed most of the facts before mentioned, and to confirm his statement took officers into the garden telling them where, by digging, they could find numerous skeletons, and in this way several were dug up. He also stated that a great many more were buried there. At the time she was arrested she had twenty one negroes confined in her house awaiting their transportation south; these were all of them liberated, and permitted to return to their former place of abode.

After this examination they were put into prison to await the sitting of the Criminal Court, when they were tried, convicted, condemned, and she with two of her accomplices was sentenced to be hung; they were then remanded back to prison to await the day of execution. Three of her gang who it appeared had not been long in the business and who as yet had committed no murders, being only accessory, were sentenced to four years imprisonment at hard labour and three years solitary confinement. While in prison about three weeks before the day on which she was to be executed, she obtained some poison and poisoned herself to avoid the disgrace of exposure and a public execution, which she knew to be inevitable; she died a most terrible and awful death. After the effects of the poison which she had taken began to take effect, she raved like a maniac, tearing the clothes from off her body, and tore the hair from her head by handfuls, attempting to lay hold and bite every thing within her reach, cursing God and the hour that gave her birth. After these fits of insanity had a little subsided and reason had in a measure again restored itself, then the pangs of a guilty conscience, and remorse with all its guilty horrors and bitter anguish, would sear her soul, and she would cry out in the bitterness of her torments, that she already felt the torments of hell, reproaching herself in the most bitter terms for the awful crimes she had committed. Then she would rave again like a madman, cursing and swearing in an awful manner, attempting to destroy every thing within her reach and so strong was she in these fits of raving, that it was with difficulty that three men were able to keep her on a bed. She appeared to be in great agony and pain during the whole time until she died. About an hour before her death she became calm and appeared to be perfectly sensible of the awful situation she was in, and expressed a desire to be visited by a priest in order that she might make a confession of the dreadful crimes she had committed. Accordingly one was sent for and she made her confession nearly as follows.

She said that she had killed eleven persons with her own hands and had also been accessory to the murder of more than a dozen others, and that she herself killed the traveller, last mentioned, and that she had been guilty of the shocking crime of murdering one of her own offspring, by strangling it when three days old, and that she also poisoned her husband, and that she and one of her gang had just laid their plans for murdering in their beds two of her neighbours who were considered wealthy, and that they should have committed the murders if they had not been arrested.

She was then seized with another fit of despair and fell to raving in a terrible manner, crying out that she then felt the bitterest torments of hell, thus she went on until she sank back on her pillow exhausted, and her immortal spirit winged its way to appear before the tribunal judge there to answer for the dreadful deeds committed in the body. Her death was truly heart-rending and awful, and should act as a warning voice to all who read the account to be prepared to meet their eternal judge and render such an account of their past lives as shall be acceptable in his sight. The other two accomplices were executed on the day set, and while on the gallows made a short confession corroborating as far as each was concerned with the above statement.

Concluding Remarks

In confirmation of the authenticity of the facts contained in the foregoing Narrative, the Publishers esteem it not unimportant, to state, that but a very short period has elapsed since the death of this unfortunate and ill fated woman, and one, whom, in consequence of the strong and prevailing propensities ever manifested by her to commit crimes of the most heinous as well as unprovoked nature, was considered by a celebrated and highly respected Phrenologist as a proper subject (after death) for Phrenological examination, and who sought and obtained possession of her skull for that purpose a few months since, at Georgetown (state of Delaware) and which still remains in possession of a gentleman (Mr. O. S. Fowler) of Philadelphia. And the Publishers in delineating and presenting to public view the atrocious crimes of this vile and wicked woman, are in a very great degree prompted by an ardent desire to preserve the honest fame of those who enjoy a good reputation, and to secure the peace of mind of those who are yet unconscious of offence; as it is well known that a cunning, artful mind, actuated by ill nature if not checked in youth, may pass on by indulgence to acts of fraud and violence and in some instances to cold blooded murder! as it appears that when even the tenderness of the female sex (of which the foregoing pages furnish an example) is converted into the barbarity of the traitor, that she, who should have made her faithful arm a pillow for the head of her husband, conspired to raise it against his domestic peace, his life! that the bosom that should have been filled with fidelity and affection treacherously contrived (in addition to other crimes) a plan of fatal destruction! Hence as has been observed, it is the sincere hope of the Publishers in sending this Narrative abroad, that it may not only have the happy and desired effect of rescuing some misguided youth from similar offences, but to save others of more ripened years from a fate similar to that of the wretched Lucretia P. Cannon.

www.ingramcontent.com/pod-product-compliance
Lightning Source LLC
Chambersburg PA
CBHW041222030426
42336CB00024B/3420